Disclaimer

The information provided in this book is for entertainment purposes only. While the author, Trivia Ape, and the publisher have made every effort to ensure the accuracy and completeness of the information contained herein, they assume no responsibility for errors, inaccuracies, omissions, or any inconsistency herein. The content in this book is provided "as is," and any reliance you place on such information is strictly at your own risk.

This book may contain opinions and views that are not necessarily those of the author or publisher. No endorsement of any kind implied by including any third-party content. This book is not affiliated with any product, service, or organization mentioned herein.

For specific advice, facts, or information, please consult a professional or the appropriate entity.

Trivia Ape

South Elgin, IL 60177

triviaape@gmail.com

Dedication

To my beloved family, who have stood by me with unwavering support and endless encouragement throughout the countless hours of research and writing. Your love and belief in my dreams have not only fueled my dedication but have also been the light guiding me through moments of doubt and challenge. I am deeply grateful for each of you—your laughter, your advice, and your comforting presence are the foundation of all my endeavors.

And to all the readers who pick up this book, whether out of curiosity, a love of learning, or a moment of leisure. You are the heart of this journey. Each page is crafted with you in mind, aiming to spark your interest and invite you into a world of fascinating facts and intriguing knowledge. May you find joy and inspiration in these words, and may they ignite in you a lifelong passion for discovery.

This book is a tribute to the enduring bonds of family and the shared human quest for knowledge. Thank you for being part of this adventure.

About the Author

Trivia Ape is an acclaimed author and a veritable fountain of knowledge, having penned over 7,500 books in a prolific career that spans several decades. With a boundless passion for trivia, puzzles, and all things intriguing, Trivia Ape has become a household name among enthusiasts of fun facts and brain teasers.

Born into a family with a rich tradition of storytelling and education, Trivia Ape developed a love for research and learning at an early age. This passion evolved into a career dedicated to exploring a multitude of subjects, ranging from history and science to sports and cinema. Trivia Ape's writings are celebrated for their ability to transform obscure facts and complex topics into accessible and entertaining content that appeals to readers of all ages.

Beyond writing, Trivia Ape is an enthusiastic educator who often speaks at schools and libraries, sharing the joy of learning with younger generations. This commitment to education is also reflected in the interactive nature of many books, which encourage readers to explore and discover new interests through engaging content.

Each book crafted by Trivia Ape is a testament to a life of curiosity and exploration, aiming to spark the same thirst for knowledge in readers around the globe. Whether you are a long-time fan or a new reader, Trivia

Ape’s books offer a treasure trove of information, ensuring that there's always something new to learn with every page turned.

About the Publisher

Trivia Ape is not only a prolific author but also an esteemed publisher, self-publishing over 7,500 titles that span a wide array of topics and disciplines. Established with the vision of making knowledge accessible and engaging, Trivia Ape has built a reputation for producing high-quality, informative, and entertaining books.

As a self-publisher, Trivia Ape takes a hands-on approach to each publication. Every book is the result of meticulous research and collaboration with experts in various fields. This ensures that each volume is not only factually accurate but also rich in content that is authoritative yet approachable. Our catalog includes works on history, science, sports, and more, each crafted by specialists with deep knowledge and passion for their subject.

Trivia Ape prides itself on being a bridge between expert knowledge and curious readers. We understand that our audience relies on us for credible and detailed information, which is why we commit to the highest standards of research and presentation in each project. Our goal is to create books that not only inform but also inspire our readers to explore new topics and deepen their understanding of the world.

By self-publishing, Trivia Ape maintains control over every aspect of the publishing process, from selecting topics and collaborating with authors to the final stages of production. This ensures that each book meets our stringent quality criteria and aligns with our educational mission.

Join us on a journey of discovery with each book published under the Trivia Ape banner—where learning is an adventure.

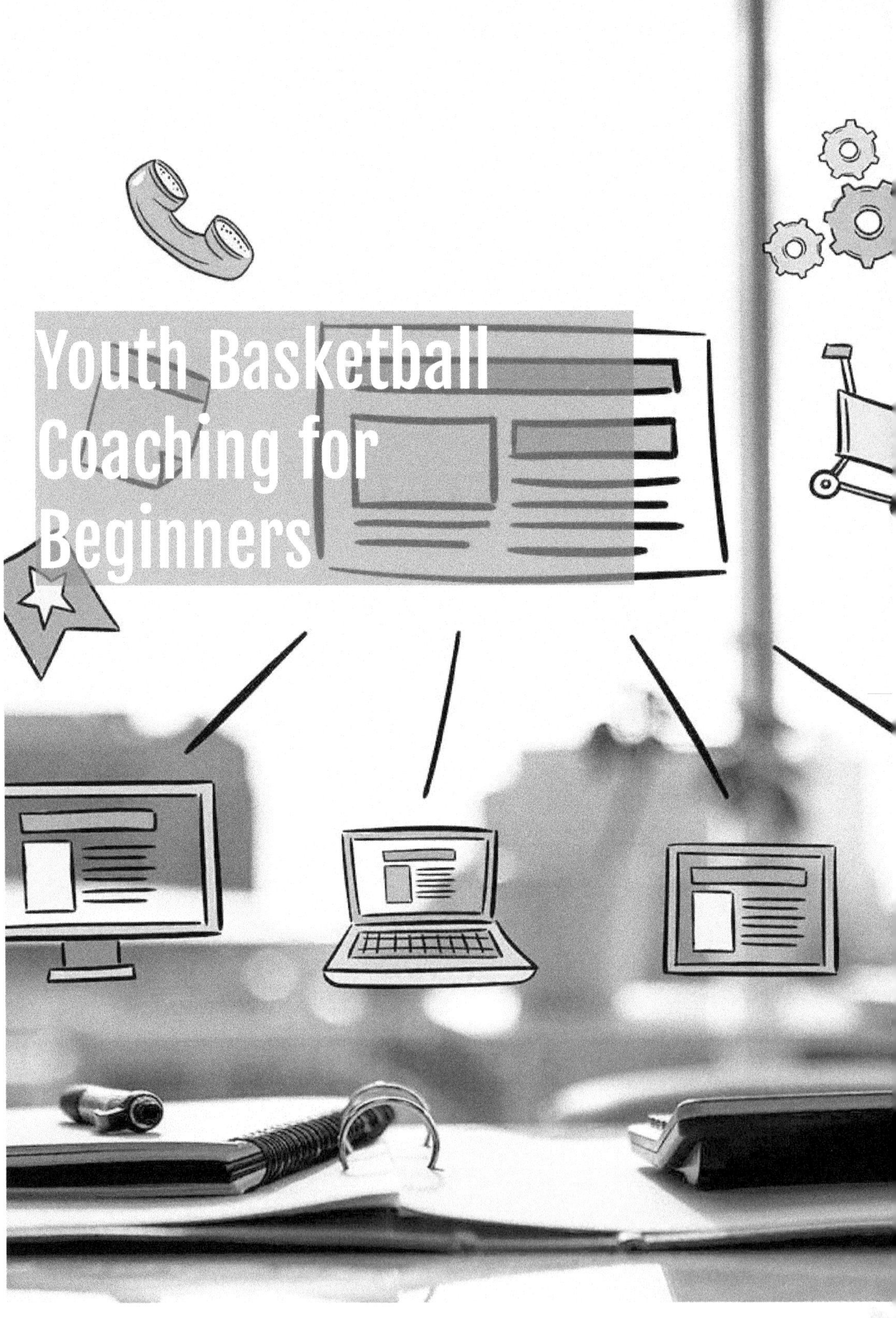
Youth Basketball
Coaching for
Beginners

Table of Contents

Table of Contents

Introduction to Youth Basketball Coaching

Welcome to 'Youth Basketball Coaching for Beginners,' your essential guide to stepping into the role of a basketball coach for young athletes. Whether you're a parent volunteer, a teacher, or simply someone passionate about the game, this chapter will serve as your first step into the world of youth basketball coaching. Our aim is to equip you with the knowledge and confidence needed to inspire and develop the next generation of basketball players. Here, we will discuss the importance of coaching, the impact you can have on young lives, and what you can expect as you embark on this rewarding journey.

The Importance of Youth Basketball Coaching

Youth basketball isn't just about teaching kids how to dribble, shoot, or pass. It's about nurturing life skills such as teamwork, discipline, and perseverance. As a coach, you'll play a critical role in shaping not only the athletic abilities of your players but also their character. Your influence extends beyond the court, affecting their personal growth and future endeavors. The lessons learned in basketball can translate into valuable skills in school, social interactions, and later in professional careers. By understanding your role, you can better appreciate the impact you will have and approach your coaching responsibilities with purpose and enthusiasm.

Setting Expectations

Before diving into the technical aspects of coaching, it's crucial to set realistic expectations for yourself and your team. Coaching youth basketball is a significant commitment, requiring time, energy, and patience. The primary focus should always be on the players' development and enjoyment of the game. Winning should be a secondary goal to fostering a love for basketball and promoting a healthy, inclusive environment. Know that there will be challenges, from managing different skill levels to addressing behavioral issues. However, with perseverance and the right attitude, these challenges can provide valuable learning experiences for both you and your players.

Creating a Positive Coaching Environment

A positive atmosphere is vital for the success and well-being of young athletes. Start by establishing a respectful, supportive environment where every player feels valued. Your demeanor and actions set the tone for the team, so lead by example. Praise effort, not just results, and encourage teamwork and sportsmanship. Remember, your players are children first and athletes second. Prioritize their overall well-being and ensure that basketball remains a fun and enjoyable activity for them. Open communication is key to fostering trust. Make an effort to get to know your players as individuals, understanding their strengths, weaknesses, and personal goals. This rapport will enable you to tailor your coaching methods to better suit their needs.

Understanding the Basics

As a beginner coach, you'll need a solid grasp of basketball fundamentals. This includes understanding the rules, familiarizing yourself with essential skills like dribbling, shooting, and passing, and learning basic offensive and defensive strategies. Knowledge of age-appropriate drills and exercises will also be crucial in keeping practices engaging and effective. We'll cover these in greater detail in subsequent chapters. However, always remember that coaching is as much about continuous learning as it is about teaching. Stay open to improving your knowledge and skills through ongoing education and training.

Building Relationships

Effective coaching goes beyond instruction. It's about building meaningful relationships with your players, their parents, and other coaching staff. Engaging with parents can help create a supportive community around your team. Communicate regularly with them about their child's progress and the team's activities. Show appreciation for their efforts and involvement, as their support will be instrumental to your success. Additionally, seek support and advice from fellow coaches and mentors. Networking with experienced coaches can provide valuable insights and enhance your coaching techniques.

Embracing Challenges

Coaching youth basketball comes with its unique set of challenges, from managing expectations to addressing the diverse needs of your players. Embrace these challenges as opportunities for growth. Approach each obstacle with a problem-solving mindset, and don't be afraid to seek help when needed. Remember, your primary role is to guide and support your players. Your dedication and positive attitude will inspire them to overcome their own challenges and strive for excellence both on and off the court.

Conclusion

As you embark on this journey, keep in mind that the ultimate goal is the holistic development of your players. By focusing on building a positive, inclusive, and supportive environment, you'll not only teach them how to play basketball but also equip them with valuable life skills. In the chapters to follow, we'll delve deeper into specific coaching techniques, drills, and strategies tailored for youth basketball. With practical advice, real-life examples, and easy-to-follow instructions, 'Youth Basketball Coaching for Beginners' ensures that you are well-prepared to make a meaningful impact on and off the court. Thank you for taking this important step, and we look forward to guiding you through this rewarding journey.

Understanding the Basic Rules

Understanding the basic rules of basketball is the first step towards becoming an effective youth basketball coach. These fundamentals not only help you in guiding the players but also ensure that everyone on the court enjoys the game while playing it fairly. For beginners, it's crucial to start with the core rules, which lay the foundation for every aspect of the game. This chapter will serve as a comprehensive guide to understanding these basic principles, focusing on aspects such as court layout, player positions, scoring, game duration, and general gameplay regulations.

First and foremost, familiarize yourself with the basketball court. A standard basketball court is 94 feet long and 50 feet wide. It contains several key markings: the end lines, sidelines, half-court line, free throw lines, three-point arc, and the key (also known as the paint). Understanding the layout of the court helps in positioning players correctly and organizing drills effectively.

Each basketball team has five players on the court at any given time: two guards (point guard and shooting guard), two forwards (small forward and power forward), and one center. The point guard is often the team leader on offense, the shooting guard focuses on scoring, the forwards are versatile players who often play both offense and defense, and the center typically plays near the basket and is crucial for rebounds and shot-blocking.

Scoring in basketball occurs through field goals, three-point shots, and free throws. A field goal is worth two points, a shot made from beyond the three-point arc is worth three points, and each successful free throw is worth one point. It's vital to teach players the difference between these scoring methods and encourage them to understand their strategic significance.

The game of basketball is divided into four quarters, each lasting typically eight minutes at the youth level. Having an understanding of game duration helps you manage player rotations and keep track of timeouts. Each team is also awarded a set number of timeouts per game, which can be used to strategize, rest players, or manage game momentum.

Let's talk about some key game rules:

1. Dribbling and Traveling: Players must dribble the ball while moving. If a player takes too many steps without dribbling, it results in a traveling violation, leading to a turnover.

2. Double Dribbling: Once a player stops dribbling, they cannot start dribbling again. Doing so results in a double dribbling violation, causing a turnover.

3. Shooting Violations: These include shot clock violations, where a team fails to attempt a shot within a given time frame (usually 24 or 30 seconds), and goaltending, which happens when a defender interferes with the ball on its way to the basket after it has started descending.

Defensive rules are equally important. Key concepts include man-to-man defense, where each player is responsible for guarding a specific opponent, and zone defense, where players cover specific areas of the court. Teaching these defensive strategies ensures that players understand their roles during the game.

Fouls and free throws are essential aspects of the game. Personal fouls involve illegal physical contact. When a player is fouled while shooting, they are awarded free throws, the number of which depends on the location of the foul and the success of the shot attempt. Communicating the importance of clean play and the consequences of fouling helps players maintain sportsmanship on the court.

Lastly, instilling the value of fair play and respect for referees is crucial. Referees enforce the rules, and their decisions are final. Teaching players to respect these officials and follow their instructions promotes a positive and respectful environment for everyone involved.

By thoroughly understanding and teaching these basic rules, you can ensure that your players have a solid foundation in the game of basketball. This knowledge not only makes them better players but also enhances their enjoyment and appreciation of the sport.

Essential Equipment and Setup

When stepping into the role of coaching youth basketball, one of the first and most important steps is ensuring you have the proper equipment and setup to create an effective and engaging learning environment. The right equipment not only facilitates teaching the game but also ensures the safety and enjoyment of the young athletes. This chapter covers the essential items needed and how to set them up efficiently for practice and games.

Basketballs

Basketballs are obviously the most crucial piece of equipment. For youth basketball, the size of the basketball depends on the age group you're coaching. Typically, younger kids (ages 5-8) should use a size 4 basketball, which has a circumference of 25.5 inches. For kids aged 9-11, a size 5 basketball, which is 27.5 inches, is appropriate. For those over 12, a size 6 basketball (28.5 inches) is often used, especially in girls' leagues, while boys usually progress to a size 7 (29.5 inches). Ensure you have enough basketballs so each player can practice individual skills without having to share too much.

Hoops and Nets

Having the proper hoops and nets is vital. Adjustable hoops are preferable for younger athletes as they allow the basket height to be set according to the age group's standards —typically 8 feet for ages 7-8 and 9 feet for ages 9-11, with the standard 10 feet used for those 12 and older. Make sure the nets are in good condition to prevent injuries and to ensure that the ball doesn't get caught up, disrupting the flow of practice. Portable hoops are also an excellent option if you're practicing in a multi-use facility.

Court Setup

Regardless of whether you're coaching on an indoor or outdoor court, proper court setup is fundamental. Ensure that the court is appropriately marked with all necessary lines, such as the baseline, sideline, free-throw line, and three-point line. You can use tape or chalk for temporary markings if you're in a multi-use space. It's also important to check that the playing surface is clean and free of any debris that could cause trips or falls.

Training Equipment

In addition to the essentials, having various training aids can make practices more dynamic and effective. Training cones and markers are great for setting up drills to improve agility, dribbling, and spacing. Rebounders can help players practice their shooting skills without needing constant rebounding by other players, keeping them active. Speed ladders and hurdles are also beneficial for enhancing footwork and overall athleticism.

Protective Gear

Safety should always be a priority, so make sure your players have the proper protective gear. Youth-sized mouthguards are essential for protecting teeth during physical play. Having a first aid kit readily available is also advisable to handle minor injuries swiftly. Additionally, encourage players to wear appropriate basketball shoes that provide ankle support to prevent injuries.

Uniforms and Apparel

While not necessarily equipment, proper uniforms and apparel contribute to team cohesion and can enhance the playing experience. Ensure that each player has a uniform that fits well and is appropriate for the climate they are playing in. Moisture-wicking fabrics are recommended to keep players comfortable. Make sure to have team colors and numbers on the uniforms to build a sense of team identity.

Miscellaneous Items

Finally, don't overlook the smaller items that can make a big difference. Having a whistle for the coach ensures that instructions are heard clearly even in a noisy gym. A clipboard and marker can help you set up plays and drills visually for the players. Water bottles and hydration stations are crucial to keep young athletes hydrated, especially during hot weather or intense drills.

In conclusion, having the right equipment and a proper setup ensures that your coaching sessions are effective, safe, and enjoyable for the young athletes. By investing time and effort into creating a well-equipped and organized environment, you lay the groundwork for developing skilled, confident, and enthusiastic basketball players.

Building a Positive Team Culture

Building a positive team culture is foundational to the success and enjoyment of youth basketball. As a coach, you play the pivotal role in shaping the environment and dynamics within your team. A positive team culture not only fosters an atmosphere of mutual respect and inclusivity but also enhances performance, builds character, and encourages long-term participation in sports. Here are essential strategies to help you create and maintain a positive team culture:

Setting Clear Values and Expectations

The first step in creating a positive team culture is to establish clear values and expectations. As a coach, you should communicate your vision, ethos, and goals to both players and their parents at the beginning of the season. Emphasize the importance of respect, discipline, teamwork, and sportsmanship. Ensure that everyone understands what is expected of them, both on and off the court.

Lead by Example

Coaches must embody the values they wish to instill in their players. Demonstrating respect, fairness, and enthusiasm can significantly influence your players. Show that you care about their development not just as athletes, but as individuals. Your behavior will set the standard for your team to follow.

Promote Inclusivity and Mutual Respect

A positive team culture is built on inclusivity and mutual respect. Make an effort to understand each player's unique background, personality, and strengths. Foster an environment where every player feels valued and included. Encourage players to support and respect one another, both in practice and during games.

Encourage Team Bonding Activities

Team bonding activities are instrumental in developing a strong, positive team culture. Organize activities that allow players to connect outside of regular practice sessions. This could include team dinners, movie nights, or community service projects. Through these activities, players can build strong relationships and a sense of camaraderie.

Positive Reinforcement and Constructive Feedback

Providing positive reinforcement can have a powerful impact on young athletes. Celebrate successes, no matter how small, and recognize hard work and improvement. When offering constructive feedback, be specific and focus on areas for growth while still encouraging and supporting the player. Striking a balance between praise and constructive criticism is key to maintaining motivation and a positive mindset.

Foster Open Communication

Open lines of communication are crucial in maintaining a positive team culture. Encourage players to express their thoughts, concerns, and ideas freely. Hold regular team meetings where players can voice their opinions and feel heard. Being approachable and accessible as a coach helps to build trust and creates a supportive environment.

Develop Leadership in Players

Encouraging leadership qualities in your players can strengthen your team culture. Assign leadership roles and responsibilities to different players throughout the season. This not only promotes accountability but also empowers them to take ownership of their actions and the team's overall dynamics.

Celebrate Diversity and Individuality

Recognize and celebrate the diversity within your team. Embrace the different backgrounds, skills, and perspectives each player brings. Creating a culture that honors individuality enhances team unity and promotes a more enriching and supportive environment for everyone.

Consistent Reflection and Adaptation

Regular reflection and adaptation are essential to maintaining a positive culture. Seek feedback from players and parents about the team environment and coaching methods. Be open to making changes and continuously strive for improvement. This demonstrates your commitment to the team's well-being and success.

Building a positive team culture requires time, effort, and commitment. However, by incorporating these strategies, you will create an environment where young athletes can thrive, both as individuals and as a cohesive team. A positive team culture not only leads to better performance on the court but also ensures that the players develop valuable life skills and a lifelong love for the game of basketball.

12

Effective Communication with Young Athletes

When stepping into the role of a coach for young basketball players, perfecting the art of communication is paramount. Effective communication doesn't just mean speaking clearly and concisely; it also entails listening actively, providing constructive feedback, and creating an environment where young athletes feel heard and valued. This chapter aims to equip you with the essential skills and strategies for engaging with your players in a manner that fosters development and mutual respect.

The Importance of Communication

Communication forms the backbone of any coaching relationship. Young athletes look up to their coaches for guidance, support, and constructive criticism. Effective communication creates a bridge of trust between the coach and the players, enabling a more harmonious and productive team environment. Whether you're giving instructions during practice, offering feedback, or simply motivating your team, the way you communicate can significantly impact how your players perceive and react to the information.

Building a Communication Foundation

A robust communication foundation begins with recognizing that every player is different. Children have varied learning styles, and understanding these can help tailor your communication approach. Some players may respond well to visual cues and demonstrations, while others may need verbal instructions repeated to grasp new concepts fully. Get to know your players and their unique needs to ensure that your messages are being received and understood as intended.

Active Listening

One of the most critical components of effective communication is active listening. This means giving your full attention when a player is speaking, maintaining eye contact, and avoiding distractions. Active listening shows your players that you value their input and concerns. It also helps you understand their perspective and address their needs more effectively. Encourage your athletes to share their thoughts and feelings, and respond thoughtfully to their questions and concerns.

Clear and Concise Instructions

Young athletes often have short attention spans, so it's essential to keep instructions clear, concise, and to the point. Break down complex skills into smaller, manageable steps and use simple language that is easy to understand. Demonstrate techniques and drills to provide a visual representation of what you expect. Consistent and straightforward communication helps eliminate confusion and ensures that all players are on the same page.

Positive Reinforcement and Constructive Feedback

Balancing praise with constructive feedback is key to maintaining a positive team environment. Highlighting what a player is doing well fosters confidence and encourages continued effort. When offering constructive criticism, focus on specific actions and behaviors rather than making personal remarks. Use the

Strategies for Engaging Parents

In the realm of youth basketball coaching, building a cooperative relationship with parents can be as significant as coaching the players. Parents are an integral part of a young athlete's development and fostering positive communication and engagement with them can contribute significantly to the success of your team. In this chapter, we will delve into effective strategies for engaging parents in a supportive and constructive manner.

First and foremost, transparency is key. Keep parents informed about team schedules, practices, and game locations ahead of time. Utilize digital tools like team management apps or email newsletters to share this information. Regular updates help parents plan accordingly and demonstrate your organization and commitment to the team.

Another critical strategy is to establish clear communication channels. Early in the season, provide parents with your preferred methods of communication, be it email, phone calls, or team meetings. Encourage parents to reach out if they have questions or concerns. This openness fosters a sense of trust and partnership.

It is equally important to set clear expectations from the onset. Hold a preseason meeting where you outline your coaching philosophy, goals for the season, and what you expect from both players and parents. Discuss topics such as attendance, punctuality, and the importance of positive support during games. By setting these expectations early, you can prevent misunderstandings and ensure everyone is on the same page.

Engaging parents also involves creating opportunities for their involvement. Invite parents to volunteer for various roles, such as team manager, scorekeeper, or refreshment coordinator. Allowing them to take part actively makes them feel valued and connected to the team. Additionally, organizing family-friendly events like team picnics or parent-player scrimmages can help build a community atmosphere.

Open dialogue is another crucial aspect. Encourage parents to share their perspectives on the team's progress and their child's development. Listen actively and consider their feedback, making them feel heard and respected. This dialogue demonstrates that you care about their child's experience and are open to collaborative efforts for improvement.

One of the more challenging tasks is addressing concerns and conflicts. When issues arise, handle them with professionalism and empathy. Schedule private meetings to discuss sensitive matters and approach these conversations with a solution-oriented mindset. Keeping emotions in check and focusing on resolving issues will help maintain a harmonious environment.

Parents should also be educated on the importance of their role during games. Encourage them to be positive spectators, focusing on cheering for the team rather than criticizing mistakes or questioning referees' calls. Share resources on how supportive behavior can boost their child's confidence and enjoyment of the game. Highlighting the difference between constructive support and overzealous behavior can significantly impact the atmosphere during games.

Lastly, recognize and appreciate the parents' contributions. A simple thank you note or acknowledgment during team meetings can go a long way. When parents feel appreciated, they are more likely to continue their support and maintain a positive attitude throughout the season.

In conclusion, engaging parents in youth basketball requires clear communication, opportunities for involvement, setting expectations, and handling concerns with care. By employing these strategies, you will build a supportive network that enhances the overall experience for the young athletes, fostering an environment where they can thrive both on and off the court.

Fundamentals of Dribbling

Dribbling is one of the most fundamental skills in basketball, and it is particularly crucial for youth players as it forms the foundation for many other aspects of the game. Developing strong dribbling skills in young athletes can significantly improve their overall game performance and boost their confidence on the court. In this chapter, we will explore the key elements of dribbling, essential techniques, and practical drills to help young players master this fundamental skill.

Understanding the Basics of Dribbling

To begin with, it is essential to explain what dribbling is. Dribbling involves bouncing the basketball continuously with one hand while moving. This skill allows players to advance the ball up the court, create offensive opportunities, and navigate through defenders. Emphasizing the importance of keeping the ball under control and close to the body will help young athletes become more effective dribblers.

Body Positioning and Stance

Proper body positioning is critical for effective dribbling. Encourage players to maintain a low stance by bending their knees slightly and leaning forward. This position provides better balance and allows for quicker movements. The non-dribbling hand should be used to protect the ball from defenders. Teach players to keep their heads up while dribbling to maintain court awareness and make smart decisions.

Hand Placement and Ball Control

One of the most important aspects of dribbling is hand placement. The fingertips should be used to control the ball rather than the palm. This allows for better touch and control. Players should practice using both the dominant and non-dominant hands to dribble. Encourage them to alternate hands during drills to develop ambidexterity, which can be a significant advantage in games.

Dribbling Techniques

Several dribbling techniques are essential for youth players to learn. Here are some fundamental ones:

1. Basic Dribble: This is the simplest form of dribbling, where the player bounces the ball repeatedly with one hand while moving.

2. Crossover Dribble: This technique involves quickly switching the ball from one hand to the other to change direction and evade defenders.

3. Behind-the-Back Dribble: In this advanced technique, the player dribbles the ball behind their back to change direction while protecting it from defenders.

4. Between-the-Legs Dribble: This involves dribbling the ball between the legs to change direction and create separation from the defender.

5. Spin Move: This technique requires the player to spin around the defender while dribbling to maintain possession and create scoring opportunities.

Drills to Improve Dribbling Skills

Practice is vital for mastering dribbling skills. Here are some effective drills for youth players:

1. Stationary Dribbling: Players stand in one place and practice dribbling with each hand for a set duration, focusing on control and hand placement.

2. Zig-Zag Dribbling: Set up cones in a zig-zag pattern. Players dribble through the cones, using crossover dribbles to change direction at each cone.

3. Full-Court Dribbling: Players dribble the length of the court using different techniques (e.g., crossovers, behind-the-back) to build confidence and control at game speed.

4. Two-Ball Dribbling: Players dribble two basketballs simultaneously to improve coordination and ball-handling skills.

5. Cone Drills: Place cones in a straight line. Players dribble around each cone, using different dribbling techniques to navigate through the course.

Tips for Effective Dribbling

1. Stay Patient: Developing strong dribbling skills takes time and practice. Encourage players to stay patient and persistent.

2. Focus on Control: Emphasize the importance of controlling the ball rather than speed. Speed will come naturally with improved control.

3. Use Fun Challenges: Incorporate fun challenges and games to keep players engaged and motivated during practice.

By mastering the fundamentals of dribbling, young basketball players will gain confidence and become more effective on the court. Consistent practice and dedication will lead to significant improvements in their dribbling skills, setting a strong foundation for their future development as basketball players.

Mastering Shooting Techniques

When it comes to youth basketball, one of the most fundamental and rewarding skills that players can develop is their shooting technique. Mastering shooting techniques not only boosts individual performance but also significantly contributes to the overall success of the team. This chapter delves into essential aspects of shooting, including the mechanics, types of shots, drills to improve accuracy, and tips for correcting common mistakes. Our goal is to arm coaches with the knowledge and tools to help young athletes become confident and effective shooters.

Understanding the Mechanics

The foundation of a good shot lies in its mechanics. Coaches must emphasize the importance of proper form, which includes balance, grip, and follow-through. Start by positioning players with their feet shoulder-width apart, ensuring that they are balanced and stable. The shooting foot (same side as the shooting hand) should be slightly ahead of the non-shooting foot. This stance provides a solid base for an accurate shot.

Next, focus on the grip. Players should hold the ball with their fingertips, ensuring that the palm is not flat against the ball. The shooting hand should be under the ball, while the guide hand is on the side, providing support without interfering with the shot. Encourage players to keep their eyes on the target, ideally focusing on the back of the rim or the center of the basket.

The shooting motion should be smooth and fluid. Players should bend their knees and generate power from their legs. As they extend their legs, they should simultaneously raise the ball, keeping their shooting elbow in line with the basket. The follow-through is crucial; players should fully extend their shooting arm, with their wrist snapping forward as if reaching into a cookie jar. This follow-through helps to ensure a straight and accurate shot.

Types of Shots

There are several types of shots that young players should become familiar with, each serving different situations during a game. Here are the primary types:

1. Layup: Often the first shot that players learn, the layup is a close-range shot taken while moving towards the basket. Teach players to use the backboard effectively and to practice layups with both hands.

2. Jump Shot: The most common type of basketball shot, the jump shot is taken while the player is in mid-air. Emphasize proper elevation and consistent shooting mechanics.

3. Free Throw: These unopposed shots are taken from the free-throw line and require precise technique and mental focus. Encourage players to develop a routine to enhance consistency.

4. Three-Point Shot: Taken from beyond the three-point arc, this shot requires greater strength and accuracy. Players should practice their range gradually while maintaining proper form.

Drills to Improve Accuracy

Consistent practice is key to improving shooting accuracy. Here are a few effective drills:

1. Form Shooting: Players practice shooting close to the basket, focusing solely on their form and follow-through. This helps to ingrain good mechanics.

2. Spot Shooting: Set up cones or markers at various spots on the court. Players take shots from these spots, emphasizing accuracy and consistency.

3. Free Throw Routine: Players practice their free throw shots, developing a consistent routine. This helps to build muscle memory and mental focus.

4. Catch and Shoot: Players practice catching the ball and shooting quickly. This drill mimics game situations and improves reaction time.

Correcting Common Mistakes

Many young players develop bad shooting habits that can hinder their progress. Here are some tips for correcting common mistakes:

1. Shooting with Both Hands: Ensure that the non-shooting hand is only a guide and does not push the ball.

2. Flat Shot: Encourage players to use their legs more to generate elevation and arc in their shot.

3. Inconsistent Follow-Through: Remind players to fully extend their shooting arm and hold their follow-through.

Mastering shooting techniques is a gradual process that requires patience, practice, and dedication. By focusing on proper mechanics, types of shots, effective drills, and correcting mistakes, coaches can significantly enhance their players' shooting abilities. As a result, young athletes will gain more confidence and find greater success on the court.

Conclusion

In conclusion, developing strong shooting skills is essential for any young basketball player. With consistent effort and guidance from coaches, players can master their shooting techniques and become valuable assets to their teams. Remember, the key to success lies in practice, perseverance, and a keen focus on the fundamentals.

Developing Passing Skills

Passing is one of the most crucial skills in basketball, especially at the youth level. Proper passing can create scoring opportunities, maintain team cohesion, and improve overall game performance. In this chapter, we will delve into various techniques and drills to develop effective passing skills among young athletes. We will also cover essential tips on how to teach and reinforce these skills, ensuring that your players become adept passers who understand the importance of teamwork and communication.

Understanding the Basics

Before diving into specific passing techniques, it's vital to understand the fundamental principles of passing in basketball. A good pass should be accurate, timely, and easy to catch. These principles will help ensure that the ball reaches its intended target without being intercepted by the opposing team. When teaching youth players, emphasize the importance of using both hands when passing and aiming for the receiver's chest area for maximum control.

Types of Passes

There are several types of passes that young players should learn:

1. Chest Pass: This is the most common type of pass and is executed by holding the ball with both hands, bringing it to chest level, and pushing it forward with a quick snapping motion of the wrists.

2. Bounce Pass: This pass involves bouncing the ball on the floor so that it reaches the receiver. Teach players to aim for a spot on the floor about two-thirds of the way to their teammate.

3. Overhead Pass: Useful for long-distance passes, the overhead pass is thrown from above the forehead with both hands and aims to cover a significant distance quickly.

4. One-Handed Pass: This pass, often used in transition or when under pressure, requires a player to use one hand to pass the ball quickly to a teammate.

5. No-Look Pass: While advanced and typically used by more experienced players, youth should understand that this pass involves deceiving defenders by looking in one direction while passing in another.

Drills to Practice Passing

Consistent practice is key to mastering passing skills. Here are some effective drills to incorporate into your practice sessions:

1. Partner Passing: Pair up the players and have them practice chest passes, bounce passes, and overhead passes to each other. Ensure they switch partners frequently to learn how to pass to different receivers.

2. Passing in Motion: Create a drill where players run up and down the court while passing the ball. This helps them become comfortable with passing while moving quickly.

3. Circle Passing: Have players stand in a circle and pass the ball quickly to one another. Add a second ball and time them to see how quickly they can pass both balls around the circle.

4. Passing with Defenders: Introduce defenders to simulate game conditions. This will teach players to make quick decisions and accurate passes even under pressure.

Reinforcing Good Habits

As a coach, it's your responsibility to instill good passing habits in your players. Here are some tips:

1. Encourage Communication: Teach players to communicate verbally and non-verbally with their teammates. Calls for the ball, eye contact, and hand signals can all improve passing efficiency.

2. Stress Fundamentals: Constantly emphasize the importance of proper technique, focusing on footwork, balance, and follow-through.

3. Provide Feedback: Give immediate, constructive feedback. Praise successful passes and correct mistakes in a supportive manner.

4. Use Video Analysis: If possible, record practice sessions and review them with your team. Highlight instances of effective and ineffective passing, discussing what was done well and what can be improved.

Conclusion

Developing passing skills is essential for youth basketball players, and as a coach, you play a pivotal role in guiding them. By understanding the basics, practicing diligently, and reinforcing good habits, your players will become confident, competent passers. Always remember, a team that passes well generally plays well, fostering a cooperative spirit that is invaluable on and off the court.

Defensive Fundamentals

Understanding the defensive fundamentals of basketball is crucial for any coach, especially when working with young athletes. A solid defense can be the backbone of a winning team. In this chapter, we'll explore the key concepts and techniques essential for developing strong defensive players, ensuring they are well-prepared to face any opponent on the court.

The essence of good defense can be boiled down to a few core principles: stance, positioning, communication, and effort. Let's dive into each of these areas and discuss how to effectively teach them to young players.

Defensive Stance:

The foundation of a good defense is a proper stance. Players should have their feet shoulder-width apart, knees bent, and weight distributed evenly on the balls of their feet. This position allows for quick lateral movements and helps players stay balanced. Encourage athletes to keep their backs straight and heads up, which aids in better court vision. Drills that emphasize maintaining this stance while moving can help young players become comfortable and consistent in their defensive posture.

Positioning and Footwork:

Once the stance is mastered, positioning and footwork become the next focus. Players should always stay between their opponent and the basket. Teach them to understand spacing and angles, ensuring they can anticipate offensive movements. One effective drill for this is the 'shell drill,' where defenders practice shifting according to the ball's position. Additionally, emphasize the importance of sliding feet rather than crossing them, which maintains balance and enables quicker reactions.

Communication:

Defense is not just an individual effort; it's a team responsibility. Effective communication is vital for successful team defense. Players must call out screens, switches, and other defensive assignments. Encourage them to use loud, clear voices and develop a system of signals or keywords that everyone understands. Role-playing various game scenarios during practice can enhance communication skills and ensure that all players are on the same page.

Effort and Intensity:

The best defensive teams are those that play with consistent effort and intensity. Instill a mindset in your players that defense is about outworking the opponent. Encourage hustle plays, such as diving for loose balls and taking charges. Reward these efforts during practice to reinforce their importance. Running high-energy drills that mimic game situations can help players understand the level of effort required on every defensive possession.

Close-Outs and Contesting Shots:

A critical skill in defense is the ability to close out on shooters and contest shots without fouling. Teach players to approach the shooter with hands up to contest the shot while maintaining a controlled sprint. They should aim to disrupt the shooter's rhythm without compromising their balance. Practice drills where defenders close out from various distances and angles can aid in developing these reflexes.

Defensive Rebounding:

Securing defensive rebounds is crucial for ending the opponent's possession. Teach players to box out effectively by positioning themselves between the opponent and the basket, using their bodies to create space. Emphasize anticipating where the ball will land and being aggressive in pursuing the rebound. Drills that focus on boxing out and rebounding in competitive scenarios can reinforce these skills.

In conclusion, mastering defensive fundamentals requires a combination of technique, communication, and relentless effort. As a coach, your role is to instill these principles in your young athletes, providing them with the tools to become formidable defenders. With consistent practice and encouragement, your team can develop into a defensive powerhouse, capable of shutting down opponents and controlling the game.

Age-Appropriate Drills

Coaching young athletes in basketball requires a keen understanding of their developmental stages to ensure drills are both effective and engaging. Age-appropriate drills are essential in nurturing the skills of young players while keeping them motivated and excited about the game. This chapter provides an in-depth look into developing and executing drills tailored to various age groups, fostering both fundamental basketball skills and a love for the sport.

Understanding Developmental Stages

Firstly, it's important to recognize the cognitive, physical, and emotional development stages of young athletes. Children aged 5-7 years, for example, are still developing basic motor skills, balance, and coordination. Their attention spans are short, and they can easily become discouraged. Therefore, drills for this age group should be simple, fun, and focused on basic skills like dribbling and passing.

For children aged 8-10 years, you can start introducing more structured drills that incorporate decision-making and teamwork. At this stage, kids have slightly better coordination and can handle more complex instructions. Drills should aim at enhancing their foundational skills while introducing more dynamic movements and simple game strategies.

Pre-teens (11-13 years) are at a stage where they can grasp more advanced concepts of the game. Their physical and cognitive abilities are more developed, so you can introduce them to more complex drills that require critical thinking, quick decision-making, and advanced skills like incorporating screens and executing plays.

Drills for Ages 5-7

1. Dribble Relay Races: Set up cones in a straight line. Have the kids dribble the ball, weaving through the cones as quickly as they can. This drill enhances their hand-eye coordination and basic dribbling skills. Ensure to keep the competitive spirit alive but emphasize fun and participation.

2. Red Light, Green Light: This classic game can be adapted to basketball. On “green light,” players dribble towards a designated line. On “red light,” they must stop immediately. If anyone fails to stop, they return to the starting point. This drill helps kids improve their ball control and ability to follow instructions.

3. Passing Circle: Arrange the kids in a circle and pass the ball around, calling out each other's names before passing. This enhances their passing accuracy and helps them get familiar with their teammates.

Drills for Ages 8-10

1. Layup Lines: Divide the players into two lines; one for dribbling and the other for passing. The first player in the dribbling line begins dribbling towards the hoop and attempts a layup. The player in the passing line rebounds the ball and passes it to the next player in the dribbling line. This drill focuses on layup techniques and teamwork.

2. Defensive Shuffle: Mark two lines about 15 feet apart. Players start on the first line and shuffle to the second line and back, staying low and in a defensive stance. This drill improves lateral movement and defensive skills.

3. Shooting Stations: Set up multiple shooting stations around the court, ensuring each one focuses on a different type of shot (e.g., free throws, corner shots). Rotate players through these stations to practice various shooting techniques.

Drills for Ages 11-13

1. Pick and Roll: Teach the basics of setting screens and rolling to the basket. Pair up players to practice pick and roll scenarios, emphasizing the importance of timing and positioning.

2. Full-Court Press Simulation: Instruct players on how to implement a full-court press. This drill helps them understand defensive strategies and enhances their endurance.

3. Scrimmage with Specific Goals: Organize a scrimmage but with specific objectives, such as focusing on fast breaks, defensive rebounds, or transition plays. This method teaches game scenarios and improves overall gameplay understanding.

By recognizing the different developmental stages and tailoring drills accordingly, you ensure that practices are both effective and enjoyable. Remember, the ultimate goal is not just to develop skills but also to foster a lifelong love for basketball.

Tips for Implementing Drills

1. Keep Instructions Simple: Regardless of the age group, always remember to keep your instructions clear and concise. Avoid overloading players with too much information at once.

2. Demonstrate First: Show the players how to perform the drill before having them try it themselves. Visual learners will benefit greatly from seeing the drill in action.

3. Provide Positive Feedback: Encourage players by highlighting what they did well before offering constructive criticism. Positive reinforcement builds confidence and motivation.

4. Adjust as Necessary: Be flexible and willing to adjust the drills based on the effectiveness and the players' responses. If a drill isn't working, don't hesitate to tweak it or move on.

Conclusion

Effective youth basketball coaching hinges on the ability to introduce age-appropriate drills that engage and develop young athletes. By understanding the developmental stages and tailoring drills to meet the needs of different age groups, coaches can nurture essential basketball skills while creating a fun and positive environment. Remember, the journey is just as important as the destination – keep practices enjoyable to instill a lifelong passion for the game.

Strength and Conditioning for Youth

Building a well-rounded youth basketball team goes beyond just honing the players' technical skill set like dribbling, shooting, and passing. One critical, yet often overlooked, component is strength and conditioning. Younger athletes require tailored approaches to physical development to promote both performance and injury prevention. This chapter dives into effective strength and conditioning practices for youth basketball players, incorporating age-appropriate exercises, nutritional advice, and injury prevention tips.

Understanding Growth and Development

Before delving into specific exercises, it's crucial for coaches to understand the basic principles of child and adolescent growth and development. Young athletes are in a constant state of physical change, which impacts their ability to gain strength and endure rigorous training. Boys and girls typically experience growth spurts during late childhood or early adolescence, which can affect their coordination and balance. Coaches should keep these factors in mind to tailor workouts that are not only effective but also safe.

The Importance of Warm-Up and Cool-Down

A proper warm-up and cool-down are essential components of any fitness regimen, especially for younger athletes. These routines prepare their muscles for the physical activity ahead and facilitate recovery afterward. A typical warm-up might include dynamic stretching, light jogging, or agility drills. The cool-down, on the other hand, should focus on static stretching and light activities to help bring the heart rate back to normal.

Age-Appropriate Strength Training

Strength training for youth should prioritize functional movements rather than heavy weightlifting. Exercises like bodyweight squats, lunges, and push-ups are excellent for building foundational strength. Resistance bands and light dumbbells can be introduced gradually but should never be overemphasized. Activities that promote coordination and balance, such as plyometric exercises, can also be highly beneficial.

Flexibility and Mobility

Unlike adults, young athletes often have good levels of flexibility. However, maintaining and improving it is vital for their long-term health and performance. Incorporate exercises that stretch major muscle groups, such as the hamstrings, quads, and calves. Yoga can also be a fun and beneficial way to improve flexibility and mental focus.

Cardiovascular Fitness

Basketball is a high-intensity sport that demands superior cardiovascular fitness. Conditioning drills such as shuttle runs, sprints, and interval training can help young athletes build the endurance needed for the game. While it's essential to push players to improve, always monitor for signs of overheating or excessive fatigue, especially in younger kids.

Nutrition for Young Athletes

Nutrition plays a pivotal role in the growth and performance of young athletes. Encourage a balanced diet rich in fruits, vegetables, lean proteins, and whole grains. Adequate hydration is equally important, especially during intense training sessions and games. Educate both players and parents about the importance of good nutrition for performance and recovery.

Injury Prevention

Injury prevention should be a top priority for any coach. Teach proper techniques for all exercises to minimize the risk of injury. Incorporate activities that strengthen the core, as a strong core can enhance overall stability and performance. Educate your team on the importance of listening to their bodies and not pushing through pain.

Integrating Strength and Conditioning into Practice

To maximize training efficiency, blend strength and conditioning elements into regular practice sessions. Short, high-impact exercises can be inserted between drills or as part of a circuit training routine. Make it fun and engaging to keep young athletes motivated.

Monitoring Progress and Adjustments

Regularly monitor your athletes' progress through straightforward assessments and adapt the training program as needed. Use a combination of formal tests and informal observations to gauge improvements in strength, flexibility, and cardiovascular fitness. Always be open to feedback from your team to ensure the regimen is both effective and enjoyable.

By implementing a well-rounded strength and conditioning program, you can significantly enhance your young athletes' performance, reduce the likelihood of injury, and instill habits that will benefit them well beyond their basketball careers. In the next chapter, we will delve into game day preparation to help you ensure your team is ready to perform at their best.

Game Day Preparation

Preparing for game day is crucial for the success of your youth basketball team. It involves more than just showing up at the court; it requires a well-thought-out plan that covers every aspect, from logistics to mental readiness. In this chapter, we will explore everything you need to ensure that game day goes smoothly and that your players are ready to perform at their best. Whether you're a first-time coach or an experienced mentor, these tips and strategies will help you prepare effectively for game day.

Logistics and Scheduling

First and foremost, make sure all logistical details are in place. Confirm the game schedule, including the time and location. Communicate this information clearly to parents and players well in advance. Ensure that transportation arrangements are settled, especially if the game is in a different town. Have a checklist for all necessary equipment, including basketballs, first aid kits, water bottles, and uniforms. Arrive at the venue at least an hour before the game to set up and allow your players time to warm up.

Player Readiness

Your players' physical and mental readiness is crucial. Ensure that they get a good night's sleep before the game and have a nutritious meal a few hours beforehand. Conduct a light practice focusing on fundamental skills and game strategies a day or two before the game. Encourage players to visualize their roles and how they can contribute to the team's success. Educate them on the importance of staying hydrated and maintaining energy levels throughout the game.

Warm-Up Routine

A structured warm-up routine is essential for preventing injuries and getting players mentally focused. Start with light jogging and dynamic stretches to loosen up muscles. Follow this with basketball-specific drills such as dribbling exercises, passing, and shooting. Incorporate some short scrimmages to simulate game conditions. The goal is to increase heart rate and prepare the body and mind for the intensity of the game.

Game Plan and Strategy

Review the game plan and strategy with your team. Discuss the strengths and weaknesses of the opposing team if you have that information. Assign specific roles and responsibilities to each player, emphasizing teamwork and communication. Go over any set plays and defensive schemes you plan to use. Make sure every player knows their role and what is expected of them during the game. Keep the game plan simple and focused, especially for younger players.

Mental Preparation

Mental toughness is just as crucial as physical readiness. Encourage your players to stay positive and focused. Use motivational speeches and affirmations to build their confidence. Teach them breathing and visualization techniques to manage pre-game anxiety. Remind them that making mistakes is part of the game and that the key is to stay resilient and keep trying. Foster a supportive environment where players feel encouraged by their teammates and coaches.

Final Checks

Before the game starts, conduct final checks. Ensure all players have their uniforms on correctly, including shoes laced up and jerseys tucked in. Confirm that everyone has adequate water and snacks if needed. Reiterate key points of the game plan and remind players to have fun. Check that all equipment, such as scoreboards and clocks, is functioning correctly. Finally, gather the team for a quick huddle to reinforce unity and focus.

By following these comprehensive steps, you will set the stage for a successful and enjoyable game day experience. Remember, the goal is not only to win but to provide a positive and educational experience for your young athletes.

In-Game Coaching Strategies

In-game coaching strategies are crucial for ensuring your team performs to its potential during games. It's during the game that your planning, practice, and preparation all come together. As a beginner youth basketball coach, it's important to understand how to effectively manage the game from the sidelines, make quick tactical adjustments, and address the dynamic nature of play that unfolds on the court. Here are some key areas to focus on for in-game coaching strategies.

Pre-Game Pep Talk and Strategy Session

Before the game starts, gather your team and give a motivating pep talk. Reinforce the game plan and provide clear, concise instructions. Encourage your players to focus on their roles and responsibilities on the court. Make sure to remind them of the importance of teamwork, communication, and maintaining a positive attitude, regardless of the game's outcome. By setting the tone early, you give your players a psychological edge that can carry through the game.

Understanding Substitutions

Substituting players strategically can make a huge difference in the outcome of a game. Always keep an eye on your players' energy levels and performance. If a player appears fatigued or is struggling, a timely substitution can keep the team's performance optimal. Equally, inserting fresh players can help maintain the team's intensity and leverage different skill sets. Make sure you give clear instructions to those being substituted so they understand the immediate impact you expect them to have on the game.

Managing Game Pace

Understanding and managing the pace of the game is another critical part of in-game coaching. Encourage your team to dictate the tempo based on their strengths and the weaknesses of the opposition. If your team has superior speed, for example, pushing an up-tempo game might be beneficial. Conversely, if facing a faster team, slowing the pace may keep the opposition at bay and prevent easy fast-break points.

Reading the Opponent

During the game, continually assess the opponents' strategies and adapt accordingly. Identify their key players and devise ways to neutralize their impact. If the opposition excels at shooting from the perimeter, consider instructing your team to focus on perimeter defense. Similarly, if the opposing team relies on a particular player, plot ways to double-team or force them into difficult shots. Being able to read the flow and direction of the game and making the necessary adjustments is crucial.

Timeouts and Halftime Adjustments

Use your timeouts wisely. They are not just for giving your players a rest but also an opportunity to regroup, refocus, and implement tactical adjustments. Use this time to map out plays, address weaknesses you've noticed, and reaffirm positive behaviors. During halftime, provide analytical feedback. Highlight both the positives and areas for improvement. Make sure the adjustments are simple and actionable for your young athletes.

Endgame Scenarios

The closing moments of a game can be the most tense and decisive. Practice endgame scenarios during training so your team is prepared. Whether you are up or down in the final minutes, having a clear plan can help reduce panic and maintain focus. Ensure your team knows specific plays and roles in these critical moments. Timeout management, clock awareness, and the ability to foul or avoid fouling strategically are all elements that will come into play.

Emotional Stability and Positivity

As the coach, you set the emotional tone for the team. During the game, maintain a calm demeanor and stay positive. Yelling and showing frustration can demoralize your players, whereas encouragement and constructive feedback will keep their spirits high. Show them through your actions and words that you believe in their abilities, which can inspire confidence and resilience.

In conclusion, in-game coaching requires a combination of strategic thinking, effective communication, and emotional intelligence. By mastering these elements, you'll be better equipped to guide your youth basketball team to perform at their best on game day, while also developing their skills and love for the game.

Post-Game Analysis and Feedback

Post-game analysis and feedback are critical components in the development of young basketball players. Reflecting on a game's performance is not only about identifying what went wrong but also what went right. This process helps athletes to understand their strengths and areas for improvement, fostering a growth mindset that is essential for long-term development and success. In this chapter, we will explore best practices for conducting post-game analysis and delivering constructive feedback effectively. The ultimate goal is to ensure that your players leave the court feeling motivated, informed, and ready to improve in future games.

Importance of Post-Game Analysis

Post-game analysis is an invaluable tool for both the coach and the players. It allows you to evaluate individual and team performances, identify patterns, and spot areas that need more practice or strategic adjustments. This process can be as simple or as complex as you need it to be, depending on the age and skill level of your team. However, the primary aim remains consistent: to provide constructive feedback that promotes individual and team growth.

Recording and Reviewing the Game

One effective method of post-game analysis is to record the game. This could be done using a smartphone, tablet, or a dedicated video camera. Watching the game footage allows you and your players to see the game from an objective viewpoint, making it easier to identify mistakes and areas for improvement.

Begin by reviewing key moments in the game—both positive and negative. Highlight successful plays as well as errors, focusing on situational aspects like defense strategies, shot selection, and positioning. Encourage your players to watch the footage with you and participate in the analysis process. This not only helps them understand your perspective but also empowers them to take ownership of their growth.

Team Analysis vs. Individual Analysis

It's crucial to strike a balance between team-wide feedback and individual assessments. Address the team first, discussing overall performance, strategy execution, and teamwork. Highlight what the team did well and areas where they can improve. Afterward, move on to individual feedback. Approach this carefully; you want to be constructive, not demoralizing. Mention specific instances where a player excelled, and then discuss areas they could improve, offering specific suggestions for improvement.

Constructive Feedback

Delivering feedback effectively requires a balance of positivity and constructive criticism. Use the

Addressing Common Challenges

One of the most rewarding aspects of coaching youth basketball is witnessing the growth and development of young athletes. However, along the path of progression, several challenges are bound to arise. Addressing these common challenges efficiently not only enhances the players' experience but also solidifies your role as an effective and respected coach.

Dealing with Diverse Skill Levels:

One of the foremost challenges is managing a team with varying skill levels. In a youth basketball team, you may have players who are natural athletes alongside those who are just beginning to understand the basics. To ensure everyone's development and enjoyment, it's crucial to establish a balance. Tailor drills and exercises that can be adjusted in complexity. Group players for certain activities based on their skill levels to make sure beginners get enough foundational practice while more advanced players are continuously challenged. Regularly rotating drill groups can help in providing comprehensive skill development for every player.

Maintaining Focus and Motivation:

Youth athletes can easily become distracted or lose motivation, especially if they feel they're not improving or having fun. Incorporating a variety of engaging and competitive drills can keep the training both fun and educational. Set short-term, achievable goals for the players and celebrate their accomplishments, no matter how small. Positive reinforcement goes a long way in maintaining their enthusiasm and drive.

Addressing Behavioral Issues:

Occasionally, you may encounter behavioral issues that disrupt the team dynamics. These could range from lack of discipline on the court to conflicts between players. Establishing clear rules and expectations from the onset is essential. Address any behavioral problems immediately but fairly, explaining the consequences and ensuring they understand the importance of teamwork and respect. Communicating openly with the athlete and, if necessary, their parents can also help in resolving underlying issues.

Ensuring Equal Playing Time:

Ensuring fair playing time for all players can be a dilemma, especially in competitive games where the aim is to win. However, at the youth level, the focus should primarily be on development and participation over winning. Create a system where every player gets an equitable chance to play, particularly in practice games. This not only enhances their skills but also fosters a sense of belonging and confidence within the team.

Handling Pressure and Expectations:

Both players and parents can sometimes have unrealistic expectations regarding performance and progression. It is critical to manage these expectations through transparent communication. Set realistic goals and milestones for the season, ensuring that both players and parents understand the focus on long-term development over immediate results. Hold regular meetings to discuss progress and address any concerns they may have.

Injury Prevention and Management:

Injuries are an unfortunate reality in sports. Preventive measures such as proper warm-ups, cool-downs, and strength conditioning can minimize risks. Educate the players on the importance of listening to their bodies and reporting any discomfort or pain. In case of an injury, have a protocol in place for immediate response and follow-up communication with the parents.

Balancing Academic and Athletic Commitments:

Youth athletes often juggle school and practice schedules, leading to stress and time-management issues. Encourage a balanced approach by promoting the importance of academics. Work with parents to ensure practice schedules are manageable and allow for academic commitments. Offering study time during practice breaks or providing support for academic challenges can also show that you value their overall well-being.

By addressing these common challenges with confidence and a positive attitude, you will not only enhance the development of your players but also contribute to a cohesive and harmonious team environment. Remember, every challenge is an opportunity to teach valuable life lessons that extend beyond the basketball court.

Promoting Sportsmanship

Promoting sportsmanship is a crucial aspect of youth basketball coaching that often goes beyond the technical skills of dribbling, passing, and shooting. Sportsmanship embodies the core values of respect, fairness, and graciousness in both victory and defeat. As a coach, instilling these values in young athletes not only fosters a positive team environment but also contributes to their overall character development, which can impact other areas of their lives as they grow into adulthood. This chapter will provide strategies to actively promote sportsmanship, establish clear expectations, and integrate these principles into daily practice and games.

Setting the Tone from the Beginning

The foundation of sportsmanship begins with the coach. From the very first practice session, it's important to communicate the significance of sportsmanship to your team. Set clear expectations regarding behavior, respect for opponents, officials, and teammates, and emphasize that how they play the game is just as important as the outcomes themselves. Be sure to model these behaviors consistently, as your actions will teach more than your words ever could.

Emphasizing Respect and Fairness

Respect is the cornerstone of sportsmanship. Teach your players to respect not only their teammates and coaches but also their competitors and referees. This can be achieved through structured team discussions and role-playing scenarios where athletes can practice respectful interactions. For example, create drills where players must work together and show appreciation for each other's efforts, regardless of their skill level.

Fairness is equally important. Ensure that all players understand the rules of the game and why they are in place. Discuss the importance of playing by the rules and the negative implications of cheating, even if they might not get caught. Reinforce that winning at all costs is not the goal, and the integrity of the game should never be compromised.

Positive Reinforcement

Recognize and reward displays of good sportsmanship regularly. Praise athletes who exhibit respect, honesty, and fairness, highlighting these moments during team meetings or after games. Giving small awards, such as a 'Sportsmanship Player of the Week,' can motivate your players to embody these values consistently.

Teaching Grace in Victory and Defeat

Learning to handle both victory and defeat gracefully is a valuable life lesson. Teach your players to celebrate victories with humility and to handle losses with dignity. After a win, encourage them to acknowledge the efforts of the opposing team. Conversely, after a loss, focus on the positive aspects of their performance and encourage them to use it as a learning experience without blaming others.

Involving Parents and Guardians

Engaging parents and guardians in the promotion of sportsmanship can extend these values beyond the court. Communicate your expectations clearly to them and encourage them to reinforce these principles at home. Provide them with examples of how they can support their children in being respectful athletes, such as applauding good plays from both teams and not criticizing referees or opponents.

Handling Conflicts and Poor Behavior

Inevitably, conflicts will arise, and poor behavior might occur. It's essential to address these situations immediately and effectively. When a player shows disrespect or unsportsmanlike conduct, have a private conversation to discuss their behavior and why it's problematic. Work with them to understand the consequences and encourage self-reflection to prevent future incidents.

Creating a Code of Conduct

Developing a team code of conduct that includes detailed expectations regarding sportsmanship can be beneficial. Involve the team in creating this document, so they have ownership and a better understanding of its importance. Regularly revisit the code of conduct to reinforce its principles and make adjustments as necessary.

Conclusion

Instilling sportsmanship in young athletes should be an integral part of your coaching philosophy. By promoting respect, fairness, and graciousness, you help shape not just better basketball players but better individuals. Remember, the ultimate goal is to develop well-rounded, responsible young people who understand the value of integrity both on and off the court. Through consistent effort and reinforcement, you can cultivate a team culture where sportsmanship is valued and practiced by everyone involved.

Balancing Fun and Competitiveness

As a youth basketball coach, one of the most critical aspects of your role is finding the perfect balance between maintaining a fun environment and fostering a competitive spirit. This delicate equilibrium can influence not only the overall experience of the young athletes but also their development, both as basketball players and individuals. Achieving this balance requires thoughtful planning, effective communication, and a deep understanding of the individual needs and personalities of your players.

The Importance of Fun

Firstly, it's essential to acknowledge that basketball should be enjoyable for young athletes. The fun aspect of the game is what often attracts kids and keeps them engaged. The enjoyment they find in playing fosters a love for the sport, which is crucial for long-term participation and growth. When players genuinely enjoy what they are doing, they are more motivated to attend practices, work hard, and improve their skills.

One way to incorporate fun into your coaching is by organizing exciting drills and activities that break the monotony of regular practice routines. For instance, incorporating games like "knockout" or "horse" can add a playful element while still promoting skill development. Additionally, recognize and celebrate small victories, personal progress, and team accomplishments to sustain high morale and a positive attitude among the players.

Cultivating Competitiveness

While fun is vital, instilling a sense of competitiveness is equally important. Competitiveness drives players to push their limits, face challenges head-on, and strive for continuous improvement. A competitive mindset prepares young athletes for not just the challenges in sports, but also for obstacles they may encounter in other areas of life.

To nurture competitiveness, set clear, achievable goals for both the team and individual players. Encourage healthy competition during drills and scrimmages, ensuring that players understand the value of effort and the importance of giving their best at all times. Moreover, teaching sportsmanship and respectful competition will help them develop a positive competitive spirit.

Strategies for Balancing Both

Successfully balancing fun and competitiveness hinges on several strategies:

- Personalized Approach: Recognize that each player is unique, with different motivations and levels of competitiveness. Tailor your approach to meet the needs of each individual, ensuring that everyone feels included and valued.

- Positive Reinforcement: Use positive reinforcement to highlight not only achievements but also the effort and hard work put in by the players. This encourages them to remain motivated and enjoy the process of learning and growing, irrespective of the outcome.

- Inclusive Practices: Design your practices to be inclusive and engaging for all skill levels. Mix up drills to include elements of both fun and challenge. Rotate roles and responsibilities during scrimmages to give every player a moment to shine.

- Open Communication: Maintain open lines of communication with your players. Listen to their feedback and concerns, and involve them in setting goals and expectations. This makes them feel more invested in the team's success and more motivated to participate fully.

- Flexible Adaptation: Be flexible and adapt your strategies based on how your team responds. If the atmosphere becomes too intense, infuse more fun into practices. Conversely, if the team appears too lax, introduce more competitive elements.

Long-Term Benefits

Balancing fun and competitiveness yields long-term benefits beyond just the basketball court. It encourages young athletes to develop a growth mindset, where they view challenges as opportunities to learn. They learn the value of hard work and the joy of achieving through effort. Most importantly, they understand the importance of camaraderie, team spirit, and the sheer enjoyment of playing the game they love.

By consciously striving to maintain this balance, you ensure that your players not only grow into better basketball players but also into well-rounded individuals equipped with skills and values that will serve them well throughout their lives. As a coach, your role in this balancing act is both a privilege and a significant responsibility, one that can leave a lasting positive impact on the young athletes you mentor.

Utilizing Technology in Coaching

In today's rapidly advancing world, embracing technology in sports coaching can revolutionize the way we approach training and game preparation. The integration of modern tech tools in youth basketball coaching not only enhances the learning experience for young athletes but also provides coaches with innovative ways to develop their teams effectively. This chapter, 'Utilizing Technology in Coaching,' will cover several key areas where technology can significantly impact youth basketball coaching, ensuring that you're well-equipped to leverage these resources to benefit your players.

Video Analysis and Feedback

One of the most powerful tools available to coaches today is video analysis. By recording practices and games, you can review footage to pinpoint areas for improvement and highlight successful plays. Various software applications, like Hudl and Coach's Eye, allow you to break down game footage, provide visual feedback, and share clips with your players. This helps athletes see their performance from a different perspective and understand specific techniques and strategies.

Mobile Apps

Several mobile apps are designed to support basketball coaching, offering resources for drills, game strategies, and player management. Apps such as HomeCourt, FastDraw, and MyCoach Basketball provide access to a vast library of drills, play diagrams, and video tutorials. These resources can be invaluable when planning practices or introducing new concepts to your team.

Wearable Technology

Wearable devices, like fitness trackers and heart rate monitors, can provide essential data on your players' physical condition. Monitoring metrics such as heart rate, step count, and sleep patterns can offer insights into your athletes' overall fitness and recovery, enabling you to tailor training sessions to their needs. Brands like Fitbit, Garmin, and Polar have products specifically designed for athletes, making it easier to track performance and make data-driven decisions.

Virtual Coaching Platforms

With the rise of virtual coaching platforms, you can connect with other coaches, share ideas, and access training content from experts around the world. Platforms like CoachTube and Trainerspace allow you to subscribe to courses and workshops, providing continuous professional development opportunities. Additionally, you can share game plans, practice routines, and motivational content with your team, even when you're not physically present.

Social Media and Online Communities

Social media platforms can be excellent tools for connecting with other coaches, sharing knowledge, and staying updated on the latest trends in basketball coaching. Online communities and forums, such as Reddit's r/basketballcoaching and the Youth Basketball Association Facebook group, offer a wealth of information and support from fellow coaches. Engaging in these communities can help you stay motivated and learn new techniques and strategies.

Performance Analytics Software

Performance analytics software, like Synergy Sports and Krossover, enables you to analyze in-depth statistics from games and practices. These tools can provide detailed reports on player performance, team efficiency, and game trends. By understanding the data, you can make more informed decisions, approach training sessions with specific goals, and improve overall team performance.

Interactive Whiteboards and Tablets

Interactive whiteboards and tablets, such as the iPad Pro with an Apple Pencil, can add a dynamic element to your coaching sessions. Drawing plays, reviewing tactics, and analyzing game footage can be done in real-time, making it easier for players to grasp concepts and visualize their role on the court. Integrating these tools into your practices can facilitate better communication and understanding among your team.

Conclusion

Incorporating technology into your coaching toolkit can significantly enhance your ability to develop and inspire young athletes. By utilizing video analysis, mobile apps, wearable technology, virtual coaching platforms, social media, performance analytics, and interactive whiteboards, you can create a more effective, engaging, and holistic coaching experience. Embrace these tools and stay ahead of the curve, ensuring your players receive the best possible guidance and support on their basketball journey.

Continuing Education and Development

Continuing education and development are key aspects of becoming a successful youth basketball coach. As you embark on your coaching journey, remember that the sports world is constantly evolving, and staying current with the latest trends, techniques, and methodologies is essential. This chapter will guide you on how to keep learning and growing, ensuring that you provide the best coaching experience for your young athletes.

Pursuing Coaching Certifications

One of the most effective ways to further your coaching education is through certifications. Organizations such as USA Basketball and the National Federation of State High School Associations (NFHS) offer certifications specifically tailored for youth basketball coaches. These programs often cover a wide range of topics, including advanced coaching techniques, safety protocols, and managing team dynamics. Investing time in these certifications not only enhances your knowledge but also adds to your credibility as a coach.

Attending Workshops and Seminars

Workshops and seminars provide an excellent platform for continuous learning. These events bring together experienced coaches, trainers, and experts who share their insights and best practices. Attending these sessions allows you to network, discuss challenges, and gain new perspectives. Look for local or national events that focus on youth sports coaching. Often, these workshops are advertised through coaching associations, sports clubs, and educational institutions.

Online Courses and Webinars

With the rise of digital technology, online courses and webinars have become increasingly accessible. Websites like Coursera, Udemy, and CoachTube offer a plethora of courses on various aspects of basketball coaching. Topics can range from basic skills development to advanced game strategies. Webinars, often hosted by experts in the field, provide interactive learning experiences where you can ask questions and participate in discussions. These online resources are especially beneficial for busy coaches who need flexible learning options.

Reading Coaching Literature

Continuing education also involves self-study. There is a wealth of literature available on basketball coaching. Books, journals, and articles written by veteran coaches and sports scientists can offer deep insights into both the technical and psychological aspects of coaching. Some classic reads include "They Call Me Coach" by John Wooden and "Coaching Basketball Successfully" by Morgan Wootten. Subscribing to coaching magazines or online portals can also keep you updated on the latest trends and research in youth basketball.

Joining Coaching Communities

Joining a coaching community or association can be invaluable for your professional development. These communities offer opportunities for mentorship, peer support, and collaboration. Being part of a network where you can share your experiences, seek advice, and discuss new ideas can significantly impact your coaching approach. Many associations also offer forums, newsletters, and exclusive resources for their members.

Practical Experience and Reflection

While theoretical knowledge is important, nothing replaces hands-on experience. Coaching games, organizing practices, and interacting with young athletes provide real-world scenarios that enhance your learning. Take time to reflect on each practice and game. What worked? What didn't? Keeping a coaching journal where you jot down your observations, challenges, and successes can be a helpful tool for continuous improvement.

Seeking Feedback

Don't hesitate to seek feedback from your peers, mentors, and even your players. Constructive feedback can provide insights into areas where you can improve. Encourage candid conversations and be open to suggestions. This not only helps you grow but also fosters a culture of transparency and continuous learning within your team.

In conclusion, continuing education and development are crucial for any youth basketball coach aiming to make a lasting impact. By staying committed to lifelong learning, you ensure that your coaching methods remain effective, up-to-date, and beneficial for your young athletes. Embrace the journey of growth and development, and you will undoubtedly inspire and lead your players to new heights on and off the court.

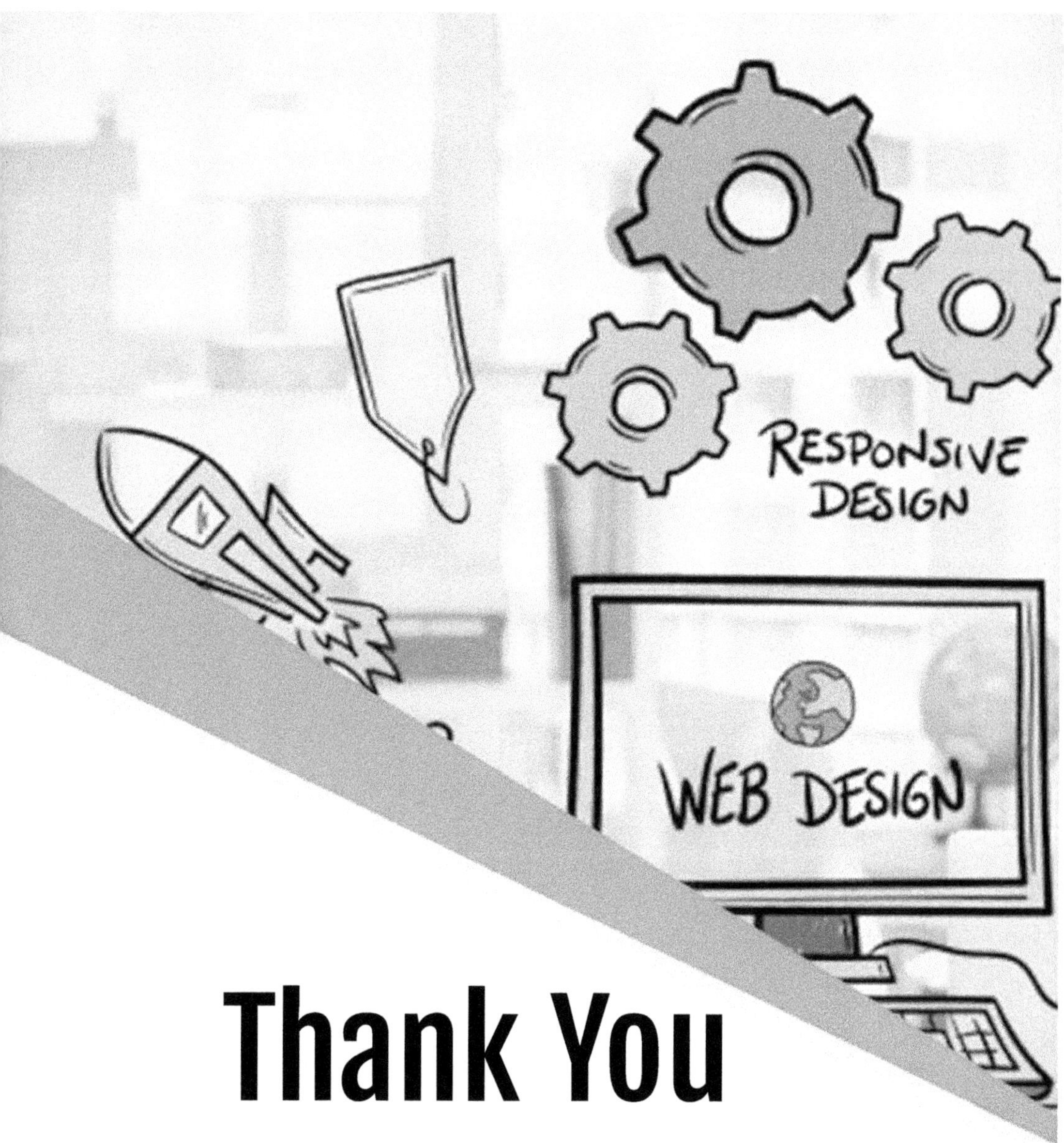

Thank You

We Welcome Your Feedback

feel free to get in touch with us for any feedback or questions

www.ingramcontent.com/pod-product-compliance
Ingram Content Group UK Ltd.
Pitfield, Milton Keynes, MK11 3LW, UK
UKHW021925190726
13853UKWH00002B/849